AMERICAN PRESIDENTS

DWIGHT D. EISENHOWER

INDIA JAMES

NORWOOD HOUSE PRESS

Cataloging-in-Publication Data

Names: James, India.
Title: Dwight D. Eisenhower / India James.
Description: Buffalo, NY : Norwood House Press, 2027. | Series: American presidents | Includes glossary and index.
Identifiers: ISBN 9781978579781 (pbk.) | ISBN 9781978579798 (library bound) | ISBN 9781978579804 (ebook)
Subjects: LCSH: Eisenhower, Dwight D. (Dwight David), 1890-1969--Juvenile literature. | Presidents--United States--Biography--Juvenile literature. | Legislators--United States--Biography--Juvenile literature.
Classification: LCC E836.J36 2027 | DDC 973.921092--dc23

Published in 2027 by
Norwood House Press
2544 Clinton Street
Buffalo, NY 14224

Designer: Rhea Magaro
Editor: Kim Thompson

Photo credits: Cover, p. 1 White House; p. 5 Library of Congress; p. 6 Arthur E Gurmankin/Shutterstock.com; pp. 7, 9 Wikipedia; pp. 10, 11, 13, 15, 16, 17, 21 Library of Congress; p. 19 Zack Frank/Shutterstock.com;

Printed in the United States of America

CPSIA compliance information: Batch #CSNHP27: For further information contact Norwood House Press at 1-800-237-9932.

TABLE OF CONTENTS

Early Years

Dwight David Eisenhower was born on October 14, 1890. When he was two years old, he moved from Texas to Abilene, Kansas. He lived there with his mother, father, and five brothers.

Dwight's friends at school started calling him "Ike." People would call him by this nickname for the rest of his life.

Birthplace in Denison, Texas

Ike graduated from high school in 1909. He got a job and helped pay for his brother to go to college.

West Point

Two years later, he went back to school. He was accepted to the United States Military Academy at West Point. He graduated in 1915 and began working for the U.S. Army.

In 1916, Ike married Mamie Doud.

Building a Career

Ike worked hard in the Army. He led a tank division in World War I. People admired him as a leader. He won awards and was **promoted** many times.

World War II began. America entered the war in 1941. Ike commanded **troops** and led an attack in Africa. He directed the **D-Day** invasion.

The U.S. won the war. Ike was awarded the highest rank in the Army. He became a five-star **general**.

Presidency

Americans were proud of the soldiers who fought in World War II. They were especially proud of Ike. In 1952, he was elected the 34th president of the United States.

As president, Ike helped end the Korean War. He also helped lower people's **taxes**.

Ike had a heart attack in 1955, but he recovered quickly. He felt well enough to run for president again. He was elected to a second **term** in 1956.

The U.S. was in the middle of the **Cold War**. Ike tried to promote peace. He wanted good relationships with other countries.

Both the U.S. and the Soviet Union wanted to be the first to go to space. America sent a **satellite** into orbit in 1958. The same year, Ike created the National Aeronautics and Space Administration (NASA).

Later Life

After leaving the White House, Ike moved to Gettysburg, Pennsylvania. He and his wife Mamie lived on a farm. Ike spent his time writing books.

Farm in Gettysburg, Pennsylvania

Ike was sick for many years. He died on March 28, 1969, in Washington, D.C. He is remembered as a war hero. He is remembered as a president who wanted peace.

Glossary

Cold War (kohld wor): the period from 1945 to 1991 when the U.S. and the Soviet Union were in conflict but did not fight an actual war with weapons

D-Day (dee-day): the day U.S. forces and partner countries began the invasion of France to free Europe from control by Adolf Hitler; June 6, 1944

general (JEN-ur-uhl): a very high-ranking officer in the Army, Air Force, or Marines

promoted (pruh-MOH-tid): advanced to a new job with more pay and responsibilities

satellite (SAT-uh-lite): a spacecraft sent into orbit around a planet, moon, or other object in space

taxes (TAK-sis): money that people and businesses must pay to the government

term (turm): a definite or set period of time; American presidents are elected to a term that lasts four years

troops (troops): soldiers

Thinking Questions

1. What was Dwight Eisenhower's nickname?
2. What did Ike do during World War I?
3. What did Ike do during World War II?
4. What did Ike try to do as president?
5. Where did Ike live after his presidency?

Index

About the Author

India James writes about science, technology, math, and history for young readers. She loves learning new things while writing books. India lives in Ohio with her family.